A Year of Sundays

Gospel Reflections 2006

Dan Borlik, C.M.
Peter Dwyer
Esperanza Micaela
    Espinoza, M.C.P.
Mary Glynn, S.J.C.
Roy Goetz
Dan Hennessey
Lilly Hess
Judy Hoelzeman
Rosa María Icaza, C.C.V.I.
Jerome Kodell, O.S.B.
David LeSieur

Susan McCarthy, R.D.C.
Richard Oswald
Jerre Roberts
J. Peter Sartain
Tom Stehlik, C.M.
Martha Elena Torres, M.C.P.
Mark Twomey
Cackie Upchurch
Macrina Wiederkehr, O.S.B.
Gregory C. Wolfe
Clifford Yeary

Editor: Cackie Upchurch
Associate Editor: Clifford Yeary

LITTLE ROCK SCRIPTURE STUDY

*A ministry of the Diocese of Little Rock
in partnership with Liturgical Press*

Cover design by Ann Blattner.

Little Rock Scripture Study logo originally designed by Maria Estaún; modified by Lisa Walz.

Scripture texts used in this work are taken from the *Lectionary for Mass for Use in the Diocese of the United States of America* © 1970, 1997, 1998 by the Confraternity of Christian Doctrine, Inc., Washington, D.C. All rights reserved.

ISSN 1554-6071

ISBN 13: 978-0-8146-2637-5
ISBN 10: 0-8146-2637-8

Introduction

"Scripture is like a river, broad and deep,
shallow enough here for the lamb to go wading,
but deep enough there for the elephant to swim."

—**Pope Gregory the Great (540–604)**

What an image Pope Gregory paints for us—a river of life that has something to offer each and every one. A river that fills its banks and invites us in, providing a place to go wading for refreshment or swimming to build our bodies.

When the Gospels are proclaimed each Sunday, picture yourself sitting on the bank of a river on a warm summer day. As you listen to the words, you begin to feel the water of life as it laps at your feet. As you hear the homily, that water begins to come up around your ankles where it may soothe or even shock you. The Word of God eventually invites you in for a swim in that river of life.

These reflections on the Sunday Gospels are part of that invitation to go for a swim. The more we spend time with Christ in the Gospel stories, the more we will feel at ease in the deeper waters.

Our Church in this liturgical year (known as cycle B) makes primary use of the Gospel of Mark. Starting on the First Sunday of Advent in 2005, we will begin hearing the story of Jesus once again. Each Sunday, the entire Church hears these same words proclaimed. And each Sunday we are challenged to make the Gospel our own.

We approach the Gospel with reverence, aware that God speaks to us through the Scriptures. We approach the Gospel with openness to hear the familiar stories in a new way. We approach the Gospel with an expectation that something new will happen in us as we are refreshed and taken deeper.

How to Use This Book

The Gospel for each Sunday is listed at the top of the page for that day.

Each weekend, read the Gospel before you leave home for Mass. Make this part of your preparation time, just as you might change clothing or make sure you had your weekly donation in hand.

After the Sunday celebration, that afternoon or even the next day, read the Gospel again, and this time also read the reflection that is supplied in this booklet. Spend time speaking the words out loud if possible, repeating those phrases that speak most to you. Then focus on the sentence or phrase that is taken from the Gospel.

Use the questions at the end of each reflection as a point of meditation and action throughout the week. Allow the Gospel to re-sound in your ears and mind and heart so that it pricks your conscience, or comforts you in sorrow, or strengthens you when you are weary.

Pray the Gospel throughout the week and allow it to saturate your everyday life.

November 27

First Sunday of Advent

Clifford Yeary

Mark 13:33-37   Lectionary 2B

"Be watchful! Be alert! You do not know when the time will come."

We have been placed in a position of trust. Before this gospel possibly pushes us into the corner of fearfulness, let us remember that only someone who is trusted is put into a position of trust. It is the Lord's house with which we are entrusted, or at least one small room of it, perhaps only our own quarters. But then again, maybe we are responsible for a rather large suite or even a wing. Bishops and pastors aside, it is quite a large trust to be a parent, a spouse, a child, or even a friend.

We are watchful then, not against the unexpectedness of the householder's return, but for the well-being—the happiness and security—of the household. The point of our watchfulness is not to escape punishment, it is simply to be engaged in the tasks we have been assigned by the one who trusts us. We are to care for those who need our care, including ourselves.

When those who are trusted keep their trust, then they watch with joy for what can only be called a reunion. We do not know what time he will return, but it will be a very happy day.

With what have I been entrusted?

December 4

Second Sunday of Advent

Macrina Wiederkehr, O.S.B.

Mark 1:1-8   Lectionary 5B

"Prepare the way of the Lord; make straight his paths."

I remember a comment I made about this Gospel passage when I was an adolescent. *What's so great about a straight path? It's on the winding roads that you find the scenery.* That memory returns to me as I reflect on this Gospel.

In quoting this passage from Isaiah, John the Baptist suggests an urgency about opening our hearts to God. Metaphorically the winding roads slow us down. Although I like winding roads, if I am in a hurry I take the straight road. Of course it is not *speed* we are advocating here, but rather *steadfastness* on the spiritual journey. The season of Advent is a time to evaluate, not our speed, but our stability in our quest for God. It is time to evaluate the obstacles in our lives.

John was called to be a herald of the Lord's coming. He was to prepare hearts to recognize God's arrival in Christ. Each of us has a John-the-Baptist-spirit in us. From our own wilderness places we proclaim with our lives that it is time to get ready.

In what small way can I help to prepare others to be vessels of openness for God's coming?

December 11

Third Sunday of Advent

Roy Goetz

John 1:6-8, 19-28   Lectionary 8B

"He was not the light, but came to testify to the light."

The violet we use to decorate our churches during this season is the first color we see as the night sky changes from dark to light. This shade between dark and light reminds us that we wait in anticipation of the light—the birth of Jesus. John was not the light, but he came to say the light was coming. John knew his own role well—he was not the Christ, not Elijah, not the Prophet, but the one who cried out and called people to a baptism of repentance.

We received the light of Christ at our baptism, but perhaps we need John's baptism of repentance during this season. Maybe there is something in our life that is keeping us from fully preparing to receive Jesus this Christmas. Without a doubt, the world will speed up around us this season, but we are called to slow down, to look carefully at ourselves, and to prepare a place in our heart for the Christ Child. The sky is changing from black to violet; the light is coming. Are we ready?

How could repentance help me to prepare for the light of Christ to shine through my life?

December 18

Fourth Sunday of Advent

Gregory C. Wolfe

Luke 1:26-38   Lectionary 11B

". . . and of his kingdom there will be no end."

The great symbol of Advent is the expectant mother, Mary, pregnant with her child Jesus. Each Advent is a time of waiting, not bored, dull waiting, but rather joyful, expectant, active waiting. And yet we are not waiting at all. For just as Jesus was already alive, already a person in Mary's womb, so Jesus is already with us as well.

How similar this is to the concept of "the kingdom" found in the Gospels. The kingdom has already begun, is already present, and will have no end. And we see evidence of this kingdom—in our experience of grace, in the goodness and generosity of others, in miracles small and large, in acts of love.

And yet it is also clear that Jesus' kingdom is not completely present. Whether in our own hearts or in the world we observe, the reign of Jesus is still yet to come in its fullness. The kingdom then is something that we are called day after day to make ever more present. With our Lord, let us pray daily, "thy kingdom come," and do what we can to quicken its coming.

What am I doing to help realize the kingdom of God in our midst?

December 25

Feast of the Nativity

Cackie Upchurch

John 1:1-18   Lectionary 16ABC

". . . he gave power to become children of God."

What was the purpose of the Incarnation? Why did the Son of God assume our human nature? Certainly it was not for God's sake; rather, it was for our sake.

The Nicene Creed states simply that Jesus became human for us and for our salvation. The Catechism says that Jesus is the definitive "Amen" of God's love for us (§1065). When

God's own Son entered into our world, he shared the very life of God with us in a way that allows us into God's family as intimate members.

Christmas, then, is certainly a celebration of God's great gift in the person of Jesus, but it is also a time to celebrate our own identify as God's sons and daughters, sisters and brothers to Jesus.

Notice, too, that we have the power to *become* children of God. As with any gift, it is in using and cherishing the gift that it becomes truly our own. As we follow the child Jesus, we mature or grow into a certain dignity. Our own dignity as children of God will shape the way we live in the world and respond to its sorrows and its beauties.

This Christmas, how can I better appreciate my dignity as a son or daughter of God?

January 1

Solemnity of Mary, Mother of God

Tom Stehlik, c.m.

Luke 2:16-21 Lectionary 18ABC

Mary kept all these things, reflecting on them in her heart.

The Christmas season draws us into the mystery of Immanuel—*God with us*. At the heart of this celebration we contemplate that God became like us, became human. By God's design, Jesus came into the world through his mother, Mary. His birth was like ours, wondrous, painful, joyful, bloody, and messy. After nine long months of waiting, praying, growing, caring for the two, Mary was able to hold Jesus in her arms. Who could be more closely united together than a mother with her newborn baby?

St. Luke tells us that in her heart Mary reflected on all that was happening.

> . . . *How the words of the angel came true in ways that she could never imagine.*

> . . . *How new life comes through pain and suffering.*

> . . . *What surprise and wonder to see how his features and expressions reflected hers.*

> . . . *Both how fragile and resilient life really is.*

> . . . *Fears and dreams of what the future would bring.*

Mary's openness and faithfulness to God, has led her to a place beyond her wildest dreams, where she is humbled, filled with awe and wonder.

Am I open to the wonders of the Almighty that come to those who surrender to God? Has God blessed me with new life, after a preparation time of pain and suffering?

Feast of Epiphany

Cackie Upchurch

Matthew 2:1-12   Lectionary 20B

"Go and search diligently for the child."

King Herod's search for the "newborn king of the Jews" fills readers with dread; we know the plans Herod has for this child who might someday threaten his power. And yet, Herod's words contain great wisdom. We too are called to make a diligent search for Jesus.

Diligence is characterized by a steady effort, an unwavering spirit, and an ability to focus on the object of our desire. It's not that *Jesus* is so hard to find—he's right in our midst. That's the lesson of the Incarnation. Diligence is needed because *we* can so easily be distracted and lose our way.

When we search diligently for the child Jesus, we discover at the same time the immensity of God's loving desire to be one with us. We encounter not only a babe in swaddling clothes, but in the manger we find all the hopes and dreams of humanity and we are invited to bow low in awe—in awe of what Jesus reveals to us about God and in awe of what Jesus reveals to us about our own human nature.

Like the Magi who are filled with anticipation, our search is one of longing. Like the Magi, our search will lead to joy.

When has my search for Jesus led me to a greater realization of God's own desires for my life?

Second Sunday in Ordinary Time

Dan Hennessey

John 1:35-42   Lectionary 65B

"What are you looking for?"

As the disciples leave John to follow the Lord, Jesus turns to them and asks "What are you looking for?" It is a logical question in the context of the story. Were they looking for conversation about the Law? Were they looking for a political leader, position and power? Or were they simply seeking God's will for their lives?

The question is addressed not just to the two disciples, but to all of us. In the context of our lives, Jesus asks, "What are you looking for in *your* life? What is important to you?" We might reasonably respond with our hopes for a promotion or to be free of financial pressures. Perhaps we would answer with our desire for reconciliation in our family or the healing of a loved one. It is logical that we would respond with our goals, hopes, and dreams. Yet, as Christians, that reply would be incomplete.

Our answer should reflect our faith and hope that lie in our Lord Jesus. At the end of the day, whatever it is that we have been seeking, let us pray that our answer echoes that of Andrew, brother of Simon Peter, "We have found the Messiah!"

How do I answer Jesus when he asks, "What are you looking for?"

January 22

Third Sunday in Ordinary Time

Susan McCarthy, R.D.C.

Mark 1:14-20   Lectionary 68B

"Repent, and believe in the gospel."

When the Rite of Christian Initiation of Adults is done well in a parish, those who participate—catechumens, candidates, as well as their catechists and sponsors—truly experience the conversion called for in today's Gospel.

In many ways, these people experience what the first disciples experienced: they come to know and love Jesus and because of that attraction they want to make changes in their lives so they can become more like him. This is the repentance or transformation Jesus invites us to experience.

The Gospel helps us to know Jesus. Belief in the Gospel demands following Jesus' example of healing and reconciling a world that seems to grow more harsh and polarized. Is the Gospel the center of our lives? Are we people who live the experience of "dying and rising" each day?

In six weeks you and I will be invited to receive ashes and hear the injunction, "Turn from your sin and be faithful to the Gospel." Though the invitation to turn from sin is most pronounced as we begin the Lenten season, the call to make changes in our lives is always present; in fact it is at the heart of who we are as disciples of Jesus.

What changes do I see in my life when I allow myself to repent and believe?

January 29

Fourth Sunday in Ordinary Time

Jerre Roberts

Mark 1:21-28   Lectionary 71B

The people were spellbound . . . because he taught with authority and not like the scribes.

In my college freshman year, I studied under an extraordinary history professor. From the moment he walked in, the classroom became a stage where the history of Western Civilization was enacted. Dr. Robert Reid engaged our imagination with scenes from the past, making what happened in Athens 2,000 years ago come to life **without using a single note!** Until then, history was a series of dry events that happened long ago: dates, names, treaties, battles contained in the pages of lifeless textbooks to be memorized for a test and then quickly forgotten. But my view of life was changed during that semester. He taught like no one I had ever heard before. He taught with authority.

The people who listened to Jesus at the beginning of his ministry must have had a similar experience. Unlike the religious teachers with whom they were familiar—the scribes and the rabbis—Jesus spoke with authority. He did not quote the "experts"; he was the expert! Try to imagine how their hearts must have pounded as they listened to Jesus' words for the first time!

Today Jesus speaks to me with the same authority. Am I prepared to be amazed as I listen to his words?

Fifth Sunday in Ordinary Time

Esperanza Micaela Espinoza, M.C.P.

Mark 1:29-39   Lectionary 74B

Her fever left her and she waited on them.

Yes, Jesus healed many sick and with this same confidence, Peter knew that the Master would heal his mother-in-law.

We could think that it was a simple fever, but in Jesus' time, fever was one of the main causes and a sure sign of death. It was a symptom that indicated that whatever the disease, it was advanced.

This passage, although brief in its narration, possesses a profound example of conversion. Jesus "approached," grasped her hand, and "helped her up." The fever was gone and she waited on them. We might have expected her to sing and dance for joy, but she uses her miraculous, new-found health to serve others.

A true, authentic, and real conversion always starts with an encounter, a "coming together" face to face with Jesus, where, in the presence of that God who can do all things, we are transformed, or "raised up." Those who have truly been touched by the Lord will be grateful for his love and mercy and will empty themselves, turning over their whole being to him by attending others, making possible the kingdom of God here and now.

How can I help show others the possibility of the kingdom of God?

Sixth Sunday in Ordinary Time

David LeSieur

Mark 1:40-45   Lectionary 77B

A leper came to Jesus . . . moved with pity, [Jesus] stretched out his hand.

In Jesus' day "leprosy" could mean any of a number of skin disorders, from rashes to what we today call Hansen's disease. Whatever form the malady took, it was considered serious enough to require the sufferer to remove himself from the community until a healing took place. Lepers were like the living dead, separated by law from their friends and loved ones, always keeping to the outskirts of villages, helpless, unwanted, untouchable, feared.

The leper in today's reading crashes through the conventions associated with his illness: he comes to Jesus, kneels before him, and asks to be healed. He's had enough; he comes directly to the Lord and tells him what he needs . . . and receives it.

Jesus meets the man right where he is because he sees him as a human, not merely as a walking mass of sores.

Jesus goes beyond the law and touches the man, healing him.

Restored to life and his people, the man tells everyone what Jesus has done for him. Jesus sees us in our leprous condition of sin, fear, and sadness. When we've had enough, he's ready to reach for us.

What might be preventing me from coming to Jesus and asking to be healed?

February 19

Seventh Sunday in Ordinary Time

Mark Twomey

Mark 2:1-12   Lectionary 80B

"Unable to get near Jesus, . . . they opened up the roof. . . ."

The four friends of the paralytic indeed were enterprising, even nervy, when they tore a hole in that Capernaum roof and lowered their buddy into the room where Jesus was preaching to the scribes and the local neighbors. Jesus did not become alarmed and scold that foursome for what could be judged as unabashed vandalism. The Gospel does not tell us who owned the home, but only that Jesus was "at home." Rather he seems to take favorable note of that dramatic behavior and the tolerance of the crowd that day. He was not concerned about repairing the roof or seeking compensation for the damages. Instead, he was quick to forgive the man's sins and bid him to pick up his mat and go home.

Jesus' act of healing reminds us of the importance of forgiveness and seeking reconciliation with family members or others whom we have offended or had differences. If we dare not break down doors or barge into offices to make amends with others, a welcoming smile and a sincere "I'm sorry" or "Let's be friends" might do just fine.

Where might willingness to forgive bring healing in my life?

February 26

Eighth Sunday in Ordinary Time

Clifford Yeary

Mark 2:18-22   Lectionary 83B

Can the wedding guests fast while the bridegroom is with them?

Fasting is a spiritual exercise. It tells both us and God that our spiritual hungers are of more importance than our physical needs. Devout people as diverse as the followers of John the Baptizer and the Pharisees would fast for just that reason. What kind of spirituality have Jesus' followers if they have no time for fasting? How much room have they in their hearts for God? Jesus—no stranger to fasting

—claims his disciples cannot fast as long as the bridegroom is with them. Who fasts at a wedding feast?

In all of Scripture, is there a more daring or surprising image of God rejoicing in people than the wedding feast? Surely it is an image to be used sparingly—one that describes only the ultimate fulfillment of God's promises to a people that have been wooed despite endless heartbreak and their many, frequent spurnings. And yet Jesus uses the image to excuse his followers. Because they are enjoying the company of the bridegroom in God's story of courtship, they cannot fast.

What a heady wine it would be, to taste the joy in that feast, with such company! Drink up. The table is spread, the cup is poured.

How is God wooing me? Have I accepted the invitation to the wedding?

March 1

Ash Wednesday

Bishop J. Peter Sartain

Matthew 6:1-6, 16-18   Lectionary 219

"When you pray, go to your inner room."

At moments of introspection or struggle, we can be both grateful and befuddled: grateful for all God has given us and befuddled at those aspects of our lives that confuse or embarrass us.

We have a sneaking suspicion that the key to self-understanding is deep within, in a secret place only God fully understands. We long to plumb our personal depths and give ourselves more fully to God. As the psalmist prayed, "In the secret of my heart, teach me wisdom" (51:8).

Jesus says that our Father "sees what is hidden." Does he mean that his Father is always spying on us, ready to catch us at some transgression? To the contrary, he is reminding us that God loves us to the core of our being, from the tips of our toes to the deepest recesses of our hearts. He knows all too well that we tend to live on the surface and seek affirmation there. He calls us to something deeper.

When we give alms, pray, and fast, we are to do so quietly, humbly, anonymously—because in doing so we go out from ourselves *and* deep within, where his Father lovingly awaits us.

Can I trust that our Father calls me to a deeper awareness of his love? Can this trust equip me to enter Lent with an open heart?

First Sunday of Lent

Peter Dwyer

Mark 1:12-15   Lectionary 23B

"The Spirit drove Jesus out into the desert. . . ."

This passage in Mark is remarkable for its brevity, but also for its emphasis. Whereas Luke's telling of this story lists specific temptations and Jesus' responses to Satan, Mark simply says Jesus was tempted by Satan.

Rather than focus on the details of the temptation Mark emphasizes the action of God. He tells us that the Spirit "drove" Jesus into the desert to face the dangers and temptations of this world. Jesus was compelled by the Spirit, by God, to engage the world. In the face of these dangers and temptations God sent back-up—angels who ministered to Jesus.

This experience of the desert followed immediately after his baptism and Jesus returned from the desert to begin his public ministry. Thus from the moment of his baptism Jesus' mission was to engage the world, supported by the grace of God.

In this passage we see that to do the will of God it is not necessary to withdraw from the world. Rather, God calls us to engage the world. Gifted with grace, we are to resist temptation and meet the world with justice and humility. This is how we "repent and believe in the Gospel."

How has my faith helped me to be involved in the world around me?

Second Sunday of Lent

Mary Glynn, s.j.c.

Mark 9:2-10   Lectionary 26B

"He was transfigured before their eyes."

Mountains in Scripture are often a symbol for life-changing prayer and decision-making for the people of God. Peter, James, and John do not totally comprehend the mystery of the mountaintop. They are overcome with awe, yet they recognize "How good it is for us to be here!" The presence of God overshadows them and the voice commands, "This is my Son, my beloved. Listen to him."

As we reflect on this passage of Scripture we might ask ourselves if we are ready to be transformed. Lent is meant to be a season of transformation, a time to let the grace of God do its work in us, gradually transfiguring us into the image of Jesus Christ. It is a time to respond more deeply to the call of God to be holy. Perhaps the challenge for us is to see the Transfiguration, not as an event that occurred high on a remote mountain two thousand years ago but rather as a call to be aware of and present to the moments of transformation in our lives today.

Where have I felt the power of transformation in my own life?

March 19

Third Sunday of Lent

Rosa María Icaza, C.C.V.I.

John 2:13-25   Lectionary 29B

"But he was speaking about the temple of his body."

When we read that Jesus gets angry about "making my Father's house a marketplace," we admire Jesus' zeal for the house of God, the Temple. We realize that Jesus had strong feelings and was not afraid to express them. He used a whip to drive out all those who were more powerful and rich (those with sheep and oxen and the money changers), while he only spoke "to those who sold doves." Jesus was in control of his feelings and used them appropriately.

However, there is another point in this Gospel passage that we need to meditate on. When Jesus was rebuked by some of the leaders, he gave them a surprise answer: "Destroy this temple." Then, to our surprise, the evangelist adds a sentence that later helped the disciples to believe more deeply: "But he was speaking about the temple of his body." St. Paul tells us that we are "the temple of God" (1 Cor 3:16). We must be careful not to clutter ourselves with worries and concerns that we do not have time to dedicate our thoughts and aspiration for God. We must control our selfish desires and take care of ourselves (body and soul, mind and spirit) to better glorify God in service of our neighbor.

In what ways do I honor my body as a temple of God?

March 26

Fourth Sunday of Lent

Dan Borlik, C.M.

John 3:14-21   Lectionary 32B

"God so loved the world that he gave his only Son."

Nicodemus is by all accounts a religious man, a searcher for truth. Still, in this earnest (probably whispered) conversation in the middle of night, how difficult it seems for him to "hear" the Good News: By "lifting up" his own son, God will bring to life what is dead through sin.

What does Nicodemus look for? Clear answers . . . some personal assurances . . . a safe, private friendship with Jesus? Does he understand the invitation of that meeting with Jesus? Will he delight at "getting" the Good News?

We don't know for sure if he does, after all, become Jesus' follower.

Am I not like poor Nicodemus, wanting clear answers and simple solutions to life's problems, rather than a shake-up in my own life? Faced with this kind of God, who loves us so much to suffer terribly for our freedom to be his children, I may also find myself with little to say.

Is such a God "altogether too much," too good to believe? Have we heard this Good News, really? Jesus' story of a God so "crazy for us" would change the way we do things too much, for we have gotten too used to living our settled lives.

How might I hear God's offer of love to me these days of Lent?

April 2

Fifth Sunday of Lent

Lilly Hess

John 12:20-33   Lectionary 35B

"The hour has come."

Most of us do not know when the hour of our death will come, or if it will be filled with pain. As Jesus approached his death, he was aware that it would involve much suffering, but that by his suffering and death God would be glorified.

28

My father died several years ago, and I sat by his side as he took his last breath. It was a peaceful death. The preceding years had required that my sisters and I spend time with him and my mother each day, helping with their needs. This was a real hardship as well as a real blessing.

During this time I got to know much more about my father and what he valued in life. He loved his wife through their 67 years of marriage and put her needs before his, especially in the years before his death, caring for her physical needs at the expense of his own health. He must have died to self many times through the years in choosing to love her and provide for his family. A faithful Christian, he followed in the steps of Jesus from his baptism to his death.

His life glorified God.

Am I happy to give this moment, of this hour, to the glory of God?

April 9

Passion (Palm) Sunday

Clifford Yeary

Mark 11:1-10   Lectionary 37B

If anyone should say to you, "Why are you doing this?"

It almost sounds like stealing. In cowboy country, stealing a donkey might not quite reach the level of horse-thievery, but you can bet your boots it would be a serious matter.

The disciples are to allay any objections with the assurance that, "the Master has need of it and will send it back here at once." Let someone try that with your car.

I sometimes wonder if discipleship isn't presented as too tame an affair today. Perhaps it is a sign that we have put a dull edge to our responses to the Master's call if no one who observes our deeds in Jesus' name is tempted to ask, with at least a touch of curiosity, "Why are you doing this?"

On the other hand, it might be just the question to ask ourselves as we get out of bed in the morning. Why am I doing this? Despite the temptation to shrug our shoulders and fall back onto the pillow, it is great to know we have been given the answer: the Master has need of us. We can pray every day that we are helping the Master to make a triumphant entry into our lives.

What am I doing to attract attention to the Lord?

April 13

Feast of the Lord's Supper

Martha Elena Torres, M.C.P.

John 13:1-15   Lectionary 39ABC

"Do you realize what I have done for you?"

How many times in our lives do things happen that we cannot understand, that we cannot explain? We think about them over and over again, and we ask our Lord to help us to clarify them, because we cannot see beyond our noses.

I believe the disciples were in this situation when Jesus washed their feet—astonished and puzzled because he was doing something proper of a slave or a servant. Here was their Master, who had humiliated himself in that way! They had witnessed great miracles, heard the wonderful teaching that was spoken from his lips, but . . . to wash their feet? That was not proper for someone who had worked so many wonders. They could not understand at that moment, that once again he was teaching them a lesson of simplicity, service, and humility. These are the attitudes that they were to have with their brothers and sisters in the future, to make it present in the communities in which they were proclaiming the Good News.

This is the way the Lord works. He wants us to understand his teachings, but more importantly, he wants us to imitate his humility, simplicity, and service.

What little acts of service could I perform to acknowledge Jesus' example?

April 14

The Passion of the Lord

Judy Hoelzeman

John 18:1–19:42   Lectionary 40ABC

"My kingdom does not belong to this world."

The Trappist monk Thomas Merton once wrote, "The God of peace is never glorified by human violence." In the garden as he begins his Passion, Jesus rejects all attempts at violence and tells Peter to put away his sword.

Jesus' relationship with the Father allows him to be completely calm in the midst of chaos. He's the only one in touch with reality. Everyone else is in a frenzy of make-believe: the soldiers making believe Jesus is a criminal; Peter making believe he is going to save Jesus with his mighty sword.

We see Jesus coming to his death in the same way he lived his life: by calmly facing reality. Jesus met head-on the conflicts, danger, and hatred in his life. With very few words, and often in silence, Jesus eloquently communicated everything we need to know about how to live.

Our frenzied, violent world needs Christians like us to calmly face reality and to love deeply, just like Jesus did, even in the midst of inner and outer chaos. We cannot wait until things are calm and our lives are in order. That is make-believe. Christianity calls us to live and love in reality.

Identify a situation or relationship that daily challenges you to act in loving ways.

April 15

Easter Vigil

Susan McCarthy, R.D.C.

Mark 16:1-7   Lectionary 41B

"Mary Magdalene, Mary, the mother of James, and Salome bought spices so that they might go and anoint him."

How fitting that the message of Jesus' resurrection should be given to the women who had ministered to him in Galilee, had traveled with him to Jerusalem where they witnessed his crucifixion and who now come to anoint his body!

Mary Magdalene, Mary, the mother of James, and Salome represent the countless women over the centuries who, as faithful disciples, have denied themselves and followed Jesus. Most often their discipleship has gone unacknowledged and unrecognized in the annals of history though their commitment to spreading the Gospel is well known.

This resurrection is a celebration of the triumph of Jesus' life and message: there is meaning to be found in suffering and new life can emerge from death.

Jesus transformed sin and suffering, pain and disappointment, anger and disillusionment into love, hope, and eternal life. He offers the same transformation to these disciples and to each of us.

These women were the first to see the empty tomb. They were the first to be commissioned to spread the Easter message. The lives of these women have been transformed along with Jesus!

How has Jesus asked me to spread the good news? Am I being transformed in the process?

April 16

Easter Sunday

Bishop J. Peter Sartain

John 20:1-9   Lectionary 42ABC

She ran and went to Simon Peter . . .

I am often struck by the excited, spontaneous responses evoked by Jesus in those who encountered him. Hearing his call, fishermen abandoned family and trade; touched by his healing hand—and despite his plea to the contrary—the healed went forth to speak his praises; liberated from the weight of sin by his unbounded mercy, the forgiven leapt in joyful freedom.

Reflecting on such spontaneity, I ask myself: am I as quick to follow Jesus, to proclaim him, to persevere in freedom? After all, I am every bit as much called, healed, and forgiven as they.

John reports that Jesus' Resurrection evoked just such excitement in Mary Magdalene, Peter, and the beloved disciple. Mary "ran" to tell Peter, who with the other disciple "ran" to see for themselves. Seeing, breathless, they believed.

The implications of his rising were enormous: not simply a rabbi, a healer, a reconciler, Jesus was God's Son, who destroyed the grasp of death. The Risen One had opened the door to eternal life.

Am I slow to understand the Scripture that Jesus had to rise from the dead, or will I run in excited faith, proclaiming his Resurrection by a changed life?

April 23

Second Sunday of Easter

Gregory C. Wolfe

John 20:19-31   Lectionary 44B

"Unless . . ."

Thomas is known as the doubter, and understandably so. But he is also brave, not afraid to speak up, and deadly honest.

The only other time he speaks in the gospels is after Jesus has decided to return to Jerusalem for the last time. To the other disciples, Thomas says, "Let us also go to die with him." Not a very optimistic person, this Thomas. No, he is a realist, a person who tells it like it is, and in many ways like most of us living in our modern culture, with a tendency to question everything.

Jesus has an answer for Thomas. He gives him just what he needs to have faith—an encounter with the risen Christ. Then, with the same outspoken honesty he used to express doubt, Thomas cries out in faith, "My Lord and my God!"

All of us have a bit of Thomas in us, and some a lot more than others. But Jesus wants us to have faith, to believe in God. And Jesus has an answer for the Thomas within. In fact, the answer is the risen Lord himself.

Is there a Thomas within me? Can I surrender in faith to the risen Lord?

Third Sunday of Easter

Richard Oswald

Luke 24:35-48   Lectionary 47B

"They were startled and terrified and thought that they were seeing a ghost."

As our parish celebrated Easter, a child asked, "How is Jesus with us today? Is he here like a ghost?" The disciples asked the same question on the first Easter day. Jesus responded by inviting them to look at his wounds, touch him, and give him something to eat. He wanted them to be sure that he was not a ghost.

Have you ever wished that you could have been there to share that gift of physical contact with the body of the Risen Lord? Jesus has given us a greater gift, the gift of the Spirit, a gift the disciples had not yet received. Their capacity to experience Jesus was limited to their senses and the powers of their minds to understand. The Spirit would enable them and us to move beyond that time and place to encounter Jesus in all of the ways he promised.

We can understand the Scriptures, experience the forgiveness of sins, know him in the Eucharist, and find him in his witnesses. We are called to be his witnesses. Our

Lord is not a ghostly being. He is with us and we can encounter him in ways that transform us.

In what ways do I encounter Jesus in the normal routine of my life? Can I sense the Spirit's presence?

May 7

Fourth Sunday of Easter

Macrina Wiederkehr, O.S.B.

John 10:11-18   Lectionary 50B

A good shepherd lays down his life for the sheep.

Scripture gives us many images of God and perhaps none so dear as that of the Good Shepherd. Just as Jesus is the Good Shepherd, we, too, can find in our lives these shepherd-like qualities. Each of us has the potential to cherish, nurture, and protect. In addition to being a *shepherd* we are *good.* Underline the word *good.* Even though we are created with the seed of sin in us we are good. God's creation is good.

Ask Jesus to make of you a good shepherd. You can nurture your shepherd traits by finding small ways to lay down your life for others each day.

And let us not be as those who work only for pay. If one works only for money there is the temptation to forget about the heart. Those who are volunteers may be the true good shepherds of today. A volunteer works for love, not money. Just think—when you retire you can be a good shepherd permanently.

When have I lived my life as a good shepherd? Do I know of a place that might need me as a volunteer—a good shepherd?

May 14

Fifth Sunday of Easter

Dan Hennessey

John 15:1-8   Lectionary 53B

"Whoever remains in me and I in him will bear much fruit."

John frequently writes of what theologians call the "mutual indwelling"—Christ in the Christian and the Christian in Christ. This Gospel reading is one of the most vivid of these analogies. While the vine and the branches are distinct from one another, they are of the same seamless substance. Our "indwelling" with Christ occurs through our sharing in his life, flowing through his word and the sacraments.

Although God wills it for us, we must take deliberate steps to bring about this shared life. We engage Jesus in prayerful conversation and in listening. We are strengthened, forgiven, and nourished in his sacramental offering of grace. We make difficult choices, denying ourselves at

39

times, to build up the Body of Christ. We accept the pruning by his word which cuts away that part of us which does not bear good fruit.

Taking these deliberate steps with a firm faith in God, assured of his boundless love and forgiveness, and opening ourselves to his Spirit dwelling within us, we in turn dwell in Christ Jesus. Then through him, with him, and in him, and never apart from him, we will bear good fruit: loving one another and keeping God's commandments.

In what ways am I taking steps to embrace my life in Christ and Christ's life in me?

May 21

Sixth Sunday of Easter

Clifford Yeary

John 15:9-17   Lectionary 56B

"I have called you friends."

We are his friends now, and friends of each other. This means far more than *being* friendly. We are to love one another, and with no small love, either. The one who taught us how to love showed us by offering his limbs to the hammers and nails of his executioners. But the love he commands us to give each other is still not so different from the love we have experienced in everyday gifts of friendship.

After telling us the extent of his love for us, Jesus gives us another example, and it is simply one of conversation. Friends talk to each other. But what a conversation! "I have called you friends," Jesus says, "because I have told you everything I have heard from my Father."

To be friends with Jesus is to be invited into the most incredible conversation of all eternity. In this conversation, creation hears just what it is like to be gathered into the very life of God—to share in the divine nature (2 Pet 1:4). Only the most intimate of friends are told about this conversation, and yet it is the basic vocabulary of Christian faith and fellowship.

How do my conversations with friends and family reflect friendship with Jesus?

May 28

Seventh Sunday of Easter

Susan McCarthy, R.D.C.

John 17:11b-19   Lectionary 60B

"Keep them in your name . . . that they may be one just as we are one."

There are times when I can hear or imagine my mother or father "speaking to me" from their place in heaven, reminding me to write a little note to my brother or give a call to my sister. If there was one thing our parents instilled in their nine children it was a sense of care and responsibility for each other.

So it is easy for me to understand Jesus' prayer for his disciples as he prepares to leave them. Just as he prays for unity for the disciples he wants each of us to be community builders in the places where we live and work.

My parents never expected that my brothers and sisters and I would always agree on everything. (That never happened while they were alive!) But they did expect that we would find ways to put our squabbles and disagreements aside in order to be a family.

As Jesus prays the "priestly prayer," he models his own intimate relationship with God. He invites us to become part of that kind of love for our God, for ourselves, and for all the children of the earth.

Where is a lack of forgiveness or understanding in my life preventing the unity that Jesus prays for?

Feast of Pentecost

Dan Borlik, C.M.

John 20:19-23   Lectionary 63B

"As the Father has sent me, so I send you . . . Receive the Holy Spirit!"

Only God's Son could love such a crew! Hidden from public sight, frightened of their future, likely suspicious of or squabbling with each other, Jesus' old friends are today transformed into something really new.

What divided them in their past—their family backgrounds, family language or accents, socioeconomic stature, distinct personalities—now are understood as precious gifts, each essential to God's reign! It seems that these men and women could not see in themselves what Jesus indeed did see—until now. Indeed, they have become so much like Jesus that they too are Good News to others. (Convincingly so! Just see Acts 1–11.)

They left the upper room for the public square. What I see too often in my own life is my comfort with the former. Yet, the diversity that "separates me" from other friends of Jesus—language and accents, ideas and ideals, ethnicity and customs, age and gender—all are made essential for the missionary Church that draws us together. Without these Spirit-gifts our little circles stay within "upper rooms," dangerously comfortable and safe.

Do I live out my faith in the "public square" as well as in the "upper room"?

June 11

Solemnity of the Most Holy Trinity

Cackie Upchurch

Matt 28:16-20   Lectionary 165B

"And behold I am with you always."

God's one great promise that pervades all of Scripture and all of human history is the promise to be present to us, to abide with us, to dwell alongside us. Perhaps this is so because God's very nature is relational.

The simplest definition of God is found in three simple words: "God is love" (1 John 4:8). Love exists only in relationship to the other. Our Church defines God as a trinity of persons. We can visualize this as a community of loving relationships. The fullness of divine love poured out into history in the gift of God's own Son who became human, and in the gift of God's Spirit who dwells within us.

We may desire status or wealth, but even in poverty God's promise is not broken—God is with us. We may desire the blessing of health and happiness, but God promises only to be present with us, whether our health holds up or fails. It is God's presence that gives meaning to any success or any sorrow.

When we sign ourselves in the name of the Father, and of the Son, and of the Holy Spirit, we both invite God's protection and presence, and we remind ourselves of the God of love in whose image we are created.

Is it possible to surrender to God's loving presence without asking for more? How can I move toward a greater acceptance of God's presence being enough for me?

June 18

Body and Blood of Christ

Jerre Roberts

Mark 14:12-16, 22-26   Lectionary 168B

"During the meal Jesus took bread, blessed and broke it, and gave it to them. . . . this is my body."

A very young first communicant was asked by her godmother, "Did you realize you were receiving Jesus when you ate the bread?" "Yes," the little girl replied, "I believe it was Jesus, but I don't think it was bread."

My non-Catholic friends often remark after attending a wedding or a funeral Mass on the richness of our symbols.

We have a great treasure of signs and symbols, of sights and smells to remind us of that which we cannot perceive.

Mass is both a meal and a sacrifice. Sharing bread is more than a sign. It is the reality that we are nourished by Christ and have our unity in him. We sing, "One Bread, One Body" as we walk forward to receive him along with our sisters and brothers in the Lord.

Perhaps that unity would be more fully represented if we did all "share in one loaf." But the unity is there nonetheless. Each time I receive Communion and the minister says those amazing words, "The Body of Christ," I give thanks that I, too, am part of that body.

As I receive the bread and wine, am I aware of Christ's true presence? Am I anxious to be united with him?

June 25

Twelfth Sunday in Ordinary Time

Jerome Kodell, O.S.B.

Mark 4:35-41   Lectionary 95B

"Jesus was in the stern, asleep on a cushion."

One night last November a 97-year-old woman was on her deathbed with her family gathered around. She had been a woman of faith and prayer all her life. She asked, "What is that light?" They thought she meant the light at the head of her bed. "No, that one over there by the door." They turned off the light. The room was dark. "Is the light still there, Mother?" "Yes." "Does it bother you?" She smiled: "No, not at all." Not many hours later, she died.

Unlike the dying woman who found peace in what might have been frightening, the disciples were terrified because of a wild sea. They were shocked and angry that Jesus slept peacefully in the midst of it all. "Do you not care that we are perishing?" But he had a different question: "Do you not yet have faith?"

Jesus was confident that his Father was with him at all times, and even in extreme danger, he knew that the Father's eyes were looking on him with love. Whatever might happen, even death, that light would not go out.

Where do I need faith to see the light in the darkness or the calm beyond the stormy sea?

July 2

Thirteenth Sunday in Ordinary Time

Judy Hoelzeman

Mark 5:21-42   Lectionary 98B

"Fear is useless; what is needed is faith."

Mark depicts Jesus as a human being with unaffected, natural reactions to human encounters. When the woman with the hemorrhage touches Jesus, he quickly turns around, naturally wanting to see who touched him. To Jairus, Jesus reacts with sympathy, responding at once to his plea.

Mark uses two characters to hammer home his message: "Fear is useless; what is needed is faith." The woman who approaches Jesus has already tried everything else. And yet, keeping hope alive, she reaches out in faith to touch Jesus. Jairus takes a big risk to approach Jesus. Jairus held a high position at the synagogue, where tradition was the rule. And yet, risking his position, he reaches out in faith to ask Jesus to heal his daughter. In both cases, faith is rewarded; Jesus heals the physical ailments of both the woman and Jairus' young daughter.

Many of us find fear and worry to be unwelcome companions. This Gospel tells us that Jesus' human nature would understand. Mark has shown us that Jesus truly cares about what concerns and frightens us. Mark would urge us to take a risk today—of placing even one of our fears into the human, sympathetic, and compassionate hands of Jesus.

Which fear will you place in Jesus' hands today?

Fourteenth Sunday in Ordinary Time

Dan Hennessey

Mark 1:1-6   Lectionary 101B

"And they took offense at him."

Imagine Jesus as the invited guest speaker in the synagogue at Nazareth. The town is buzzing with anticipation. A local boy—Mary's son!—is fast becoming a respected and eloquent rabbi. Many turn out to hear his message of comfort and consolation. They anticipate his approval and appreciation for their strong faith. After all, he was one of their own—a brother, a friend.

He speaks, instead, as a prophet. His words are a challenge. He expects them to change! How dare he speak in that manner! Who does he think he is?

How often do we behave like these Nazoreans? As our brother and friend, Jesus reassures and cheers us. We draw near to him, straining to hear all those soothing words. Jesus is also our priest, prophet, and king. Do we listen as closely to his prophetic words, those that call us to conversion and ministry? Do we inch closer to him when he asks us to risk leaving our comfort zone or do we "take offense" and move away?

God provides us with all we need to answer Christ's prophetic call. When we trust in him we can answer the call to true discipleship. Never let Jesus be amazed at our lack of faith.

When have I felt the call of Jesus to leave my comfort zone?

July 16

Fifteenth Sunday in Ordinary Time

Tom Stehlik, C.M.

Mark 6:7-13   Lectionary 104B

Jesus summoned the Twelve and began to send them out two by two, and gave them authority over unclean spirits. He instructed them to take nothing for the journey but a walking stick—no food, no sack, no money in their belts.

One day two Mormon missionaries knocked on my door. We talked briefly and then I identified myself as a missionary priest. One of them told me that he was nearing the end of a two-year experience in mission in Arkansas. I asked him what he would remember from his experience of having left home and loved ones. He said to me, "I will never forget who I am. I am a missionary."

That stuck with me. Whether I am at home or far away, my call is to be a messenger of Good News. A basic, fundamental aspect of discipleship is that we are called and sent out. A missionary is a believer who shares in the life and mission of Jesus.

Jesus strictly commands his disciples to travel light. This makes the source of their authority and power most apparent—it is God who has the power to change hearts, who has authority over evil, and who heals and forgives. God has us to put the flesh and bones on the Good News.

Am I a messenger of the Good News? Who are people of witness that strengthen my faith?

July 23

Sixteenth Sunday in Ordinary Time

Peter Dwyer

Mark 6:30-34   Lectionary 107B

". . . for they were like sheep without a shepherd"

I used to think of this biblical image of sheep and shepherd as something akin to Mary and her little lamb. But sheep are actually dull-witted and timid. They do not follow. They have to be driven. Without a shepherd they will kill a pasture by over-grazing. They easily get lost. They are vulnerable to predators. Not so nice to be compared to sheep.

What then is the point of this comparison? Like the people of Galilee we are hungry for the meaning of life. And also like the people of Galilee we want easy, immediate answers. Some wanted a Messiah to overthrow Roman rule and establish a new political kingdom on earth. Instead Jesus taught them how to believe in a new kind of kingdom.

More than two thousand years later we still struggle to understand what Jesus teaches us. We need the shepherd to guide us, teach us, and push us. Perhaps most difficult is for us to recognize that our ability to reason has limits. In matters of faith we have to surrender our ego to the mystery of God. We will always be sheep in need of the shepherd.

Where in my life am I in need of God's direction?

July 30

Seventeenth Sunday in Ordinary Time

Mary Glynn, s.j.c.

John 6:1-15   Lectionary 110B

"There is a boy here who has five barley loaves and two fish, but what good are these for so many?"

Sharing a meal with someone allows us to be open to a relationship. In the Scriptures Jesus shares a meal with others not just to satisfy their physical hunger but also to invite them into intimacy and at times to offer them reconciliation.

In today's Gospel Jesus takes a small amount of food and feeds a large crowd. He does so because a lad is willing to share what little he has for the good of the community assembled. No one is excluded. Not only is there enough to feed everyone but there is an abundance left over, "twelve baskets full of pieces."

Perhaps this Gospel is asking us to be like the lad, willing to use our gifts no matter how insignificant they seem for others. When we do that our gifts are multiplied a thousand fold, and having touched others there is still an abundance left over to be used again and again.

Each time we celebrate the Eucharist and partake of the bread blessed and broken, we are invited into a deeper intimacy with Jesus. We are also challenged not to keep what we have received for ourselves but to be willing to be Eucharist for others.

How might I be Eucharist for others?

August 6

Transfiguration

Roy Goetz

Mark 9:2-10   Lectionary 614

**Then Peter said to Jesus in reply, "Rabbi, it is good that
we are here!"**

We have probably all had times in our lives when things
were so good, so peaceful, that we wanted to freeze time
and stay right in the moment. We might recall special times
like this—a childhood memory, perhaps a marriage, or the
birth of a child or grandchild.

Maybe like Peter, James, and John we have had a mountaintop experience of God in our life. We want to sustain
the wonder and joy of these times, "to make tents," but we
cannot stay in these moments. We need these times to
strengthen us just as the disciples did, but to plant our feet
immovably in a single experience of God would be to deny
ourselves the rest of the journey God requires of us.

Jesus came down the mountain because he knew that his
journey was not over. We may doubt, hesitate, and even
fear, but we continue our journey knowing that Jesus
promised to be with us all our days. Our Father's words,
"This is my beloved Son, listen to him," are for us. We have
only to listen and take the next step.

What "mountaintop" experiences continue to sustain me when I feel weary or afraid? How could these experiences strengthen me in my continuing spiritual journey?

August 13

Nineteenth Sunday in Ordinary Time

Clifford Yeary

John 6:41-51   Lectionary 116B

"Is this not Jesus, the son of Joseph?"

Those who knew Jesus as that villager who lived just down the lane were hard pressed to count his words as the teaching of God. What could he say that hasn't been said before? But, then, he tells them he is the bread that comes down from heaven. What kind of talk is that coming from a child of that Joseph and Mary?

It was entirely possible to be too familiar with Jesus. Those who knew Jesus from childhood knew too much about him to have any need for what he said, let alone to drop their livelihoods and follow him. They were not hungry enough to recognize the aroma of fresh baked bread.

Today Christians who have frequently pondered the message of chapter 6 of John argue whether Jesus was referring to the Eucharist or his teaching when speaking of himself as bread. And the answer, of course, is that we are wrong. If we were hungry enough for the bread of which he spoke, we would recognize it whenever, wherever it was offered. Our mouths would be full of bread, who would have time to argue?

How hungry am I for what Jesus offers me in word and sacrament?

August 20

Twentieth Sunday in Ordinary Time

Susan McCarthy, R.D.C.

John 6:51-58   Lectionary 119D

"I am the living bread . . . whoever eats this bread will live forever."

It seems to me that the way we approach and receive the Eucharist speaks volumes about its meaning for us in our lives. There is real sign value here!

Another action that speaks volumes is how we act once we have received and eaten this bread.

Imagine a non-believer coming into our church for the first time and seeing people quietly and reverently lining up to receive a small piece of bread and a sip of wine. This bread is living bread—true food and true drink. It is bread that nourishes and changes us so that we become what we eat. We become Eucharist for others.

The story is told of a catechist who was meeting with an adult preparing for the sacrament of the Eucharist. The catechist was explaining our belief that Jesus is really present in the Eucharist. The man he was instructing seemed confused and when the catechist asked what he did not understand, the man replied, "If you really believed that Jesus was present in the bread, wouldn't you be more loving and respectful toward each other?"

How is my life being transformed each time I receive the Eucharist? Is there evidence that others can see?

August 27

Twenty-first Sunday in Ordinary Time

Gregory C. Wolfe

John 6:60-69   Lectionary 122B

"Master, to whom shall we go?"

Jesus had poured out his heart to the crowd. He had shared with them some of the deepest mysteries about who he was, where he had come from, the eternal life he would offer through his flesh and blood. And no one understood him.

The Jews quarreled among themselves and expressed their disgust at the idea of eating flesh and drinking human blood. Many of Jesus' own disciples murmured that they could not accept such hard teachings and decided to follow Jesus no more. And what of the apostles? They did not understand either!

Peter, speaking for the Twelve, did not say that he understood Jesus any better than the others gathered that day at the lakeside town of Capernaum. He did not say, "Oh, we understand you are talking about your future sacrifice at Calvary and the mystery of the Eucharist that will allow us to share in your very body and blood."

No, Peter in his usual straightforward simplicity responded: "Where else would we go for answers, Master? We believe in you—you! Not that we understand every mystery or can fully explain every teaching, but our faith is in you. And with you, we will stay."

Does my faith depend on understanding all there is to know about Jesus and his life? Or does my faith rest in a growing relationship with him?

September 3

Twenty-second Sunday in Ordinary Time

Rosa María Icaza, C.C.V.I.

Mark 7:1-8, 14-15, 21-23   Lectionary 125B

"This people honors me with their lips, but their hearts are far from me."

There is a television show entitled "Keeping Up Appearances." It is a satire. Yet many people identify with the characters because we realize that sometimes we are more concerned about what others think of us than how we truly are before God. We pay great attention to behaviors and customs that are popular and accepted instead of acting on principles and conviction.

This tendency leads us even to be "funny" in our prayer life and in our relationship with God. We may go to church and we may wear a medal or cross because it is fashionable. We say certain prayers and practice some devotions because our friends do that. There is no knowledge of the meaning and importance of that practice, but everyone does it.

We see the outside, God sees the inside. Our thoughts and our words reveal what is in our hearts: "The things that come out from within are what defile" (7:16). Honesty and gratitude are beautiful characteristics of a person that speaks from the heart and not simply utters sayings that may seem proper but are not sincere. "It is only with the heart that one can see rightly; what is essential is invisible to the eye," said the fox to the Little Prince. That is what really counts.

Has my concern for appearances clouded my commitment to God's ways?

Twenty-third Sunday in Ordinary Time

Mark Twomey

Mark 7:31-37   Lectionary 128B

He has done all things well.

Jesus had a lot of common sense, which we know is regrettably not all that common in the human family. Jesus knew that the witnesses to his *Ephphatha* moment of making the deaf and mute man hear and speak would not follow his bidding and be mum about it. Good news travels fast. He realized that the crowd would tell the tale of that miracle far beyond the district of the Decapolis.

Let us, too, be attentive and have our ears open to the message of the Gospel. We should daily, like Jesus, help family members and neighbors with chores, extend warm greetings and kind words. On a strictly human level, we can also have mini-*Ephphatha* moments right in our neighborhoods and workplaces where we, through good works, help others. It may be donating to the victims of an earthly disaster, or having lunch with a lonely colleague, or helping a son or daughter with a math assignment. Such responses may not garner shouts of astonishment, but we will have the self-assurance of trying to do "all things well."

What events have helped me to open my ears to the Gospel message?

Twenty-fourth Sunday in Ordinary Time

Judy Hoelzeman

Mark 8:27-35   Lectionary 131B

. . . the Son of Man must suffer greatly.

This Gospel speaks to me about vulnerability—about the way Jesus preached it and the way we reject it.

Jesus asks his disciples, "Who do you say that I am?" Peter answers, "You are the Messiah." Peter's answer sounds right. But Jesus knows that Peter wants the Messiah to be strong and powerful enough to free the Hebrew people from the Romans and lead the Jews to their destiny. Jesus himself understands his role quite differently. He knows his destiny as Messiah holds rejection, suffering, and death.

After this scene, there is a turning point in Mark's Gospel. From now on, Jesus will be trying to make the disciples (and us) understand that not only will he suffer and die, but that anyone who wants to be a true follower will have to do the same.

Another question, "What kind of Messiah will Jesus be?" has now been answered. As Messiah, Jesus will accept his Father's will, becoming vulnerable and completely powerless at the end.

The more we can stand to be vulnerable and powerless in life, the better we will be ready to step across to death.

Maybe vulnerability is the "cross" that Jesus, the Messiah, is asking us to bear.

Can I allow myself to be vulnerable? What might I gain by letting go of the need to control?

September 24

Twenty-fifth Sunday in Ordinary Time

Martha Elena Torres, M.C.P.

Mark 9:30-37   Lectionary 134B

"What were you arguing about on the way?"

When I was in school I liked to talk a lot, and in general my bad grades were in consequence to my bad behavior. If the teacher approached me and caught me talking, I got scared and didn't know what to respond. I think the same happened with the apostles when Jesus asked them, "What were you arguing about on the way?"

They answered absolutely nothing, since it was difficult to reveal the desire to hold the first places, to be the greatest of the disciples. Jesus, as a great teacher, clarifies who is the greatest. Whoever serves others, whoever is simple as a child, whoever finds him in the less fortunate, in those who suffer, in those who are weak, in those who cannot defend themselves, he will be the first one, the greatest in the

Kingdom of God. More important is that we receive him and his Father.

May our desire in life be to serve our brothers and sisters, especially those closer to us: our husband, wife, children, coworkers, and our fellow parishioners, and do this with only the wish of receiving him and giving praise to Jesus and our Father.

What do my desires reveal about my relationship with Jesus?

October 1

Twenty-sixth Sunday in Ordinary Time

Roy Goetz

Mark 9:38-43, 45, 47-48   Lectionary 137B

"And if your foot causes you to sin, cut it off."

I had a friend in high school who lost his leg in a motorcycle accident. At first, the doctors thought it might be possible to save his leg, but to save his life the leg had to be amputated. My friend's life changed forever, but he adjusted well and continues to live with passion and a wonderful sense of humor. One of my fondest memories is of swimming with him in a Missouri stream and listening as he teased passing canoeists about the dangers of sharks in the river.

Perhaps we have known someone whose illness made it necessary to have a diseased part of his or her body removed in order to preserve life. Self-preservation is a strong instinct. Sometimes extraordinary efforts are made to preserve physical life.

How strong is our drive to sustain our spiritual life? Can we describe our efforts as extraordinary? For most of us, it would only take a small bit of introspection to identify something in our life that needs to go—something we need to cut away.

What are we willing to remove from our life in the here and now in order to enter into the Kingdom of God?

October 8

Twenty-seventh Sunday in Ordinary Time

Judy Hoelzeman

Mark 10:2-16   Lectionary 140B

From the beginning of creation, God made them male and female.

The discussion in today's Gospel is about more than marriage. It is about women and how Jesus respected them. Jesus taught, by word and example, that women were equal to men in the sight of God. Going against the prevailing Hebrew customs of the day, Jesus looked on women, not as property, but as people.

Knowing that Hebrew law concerning divorce often discriminated against women and left them alone and unsupported, Jesus deliberately moves from debating the legalities to talking about something deeper—God's purpose for marriage. The Church, following Jesus' teaching, sets forth the ideal of marriage as a lifelong commitment. At the same time, the Church realizes that, in practice, not everyone lives up to that ideal.

People in many circumstances will hear today's Gospel. Those whose marriages have failed despite their best efforts can rest assured of God's forgiveness. Those who are working hard at their marriages, but find it a lonely struggle, should hear that the Lord will strengthen their efforts.

And, no matter what our circumstances, we all can count on the fact that respect for *both* women and men is a constant of Jesus' teaching.

How do your commitments to others help you to grow in respect for them as well?

Twenty-eighth Sunday in Ordinary Time

Lilly Hess

Mark 10:17-30   Lectionary 143B

Jesus, looking at him, loved him and said . . .
"Go, sell . . . give . . . come, follow me."

Many say this story of the rich young man is the saddest story in the Gospel, and I would agree. He runs to Jesus with so much enthusiasm and falls to his knees at Jesus' feet. Raising his eyes to Jesus he asks, "Good teacher, what must I do to inherit eternal life?" It's evident that he's heard about Jesus and about this new kingdom of God. Today he has his chance and finds Jesus at last. His inheritance has given him status in this life, but he wants to be part of this kingdom of which Jesus speaks.

But Jesus has a challenge for the man. Eternal life is a gift of God and obeying the commandments is only the beginning of accepting that gift. Jesus, looking at him with love, asks him to leave all and "follow me." Not the response the man expected. The face so full of joy now falls, and he turns and walks away from Jesus. Being part of God's kingdom means putting God first and the man seems torn because he treasures his status and wealth.

This story deserves to be heard with new ears each time we hear it. It's not just about the rich man, it's about us.

Again and again, Jesus is looking with love at me and asking, "Am I first in your life?"

What would it mean to make Jesus first in my life?

October 22

Twenty-ninth Sunday in Ordinary Time

Cackie Upchurch

Mark 10:35-45   Lectionary 146B

"Whoever wishes to be great among you will be your servant."

"Be careful what you wish for" is a fitting lesson for these sons of Zebedee. They discover that in the kingdom Jesus establishes, their wish for power will not lead to honor and glory. True greatness is manifest in service.

The Son of God himself was a model of service—coming not to be served but to serve and give his life as a ransom for many (Mark 10:45), identifying himself as one who serves at table (Luke 22:27), and washing the dirty feet of his followers (John 13:1-20). Followers of Jesus are to be shaped in his image.

True greatness, then, is found in feeding the hungry, giving drink to the thirsty, welcoming the stranger, clothing the naked, caring for the ill, and visiting the imprisoned (see Matt 25:31-46). Do we wish for these opportunities in our heart of hearts? Are we prepared to feed and welcome and clothe those who may never find a voice for themselves in our halls of power? Those with whom "rubbing elbows" would bring no prestige?

In the midst of the church's "ordinary time" we are asked to see greatness in ordinary people and ordinary actions.

What is my deepest desire? Can I ask God to continue transforming me and my desires?

October 29

Thirtieth Sunday in Ordinary

Jerre Roberts

Mark 10:46-52   Lectionary 149B

"What do you want me to do for you?"

When the blind Bartimaeus approached Jesus, the last thing he probably expected from Jesus was this question. Surely it would have been obvious to Jesus that Bartimaeus could not see. Surely there would have been whisperings among the crowd of his plight. Jesus must have known that those vacant, empty eyes yearned for sight.

But first, there was that question: "What do you want me to do for you?"

It is a question we might ask of ourselves, especially when our days seem slightly out of focus. What do I want

Jesus to do for me? What is my heart's desire? The issue is not that Jesus does not know what I need, but do I know what I really want?

Bartimaeus may have always dreamed what he would do if he was sighted. He may have had hopes and dreams of leading an ordinary life, of having a wife and children, of livng a blessed ordinary life much like you and I. But once he receives his sight, a new aspiration leads him forward— a desire to follow Jesus.

Bartimaeus received more than he asked for. With physical sight he was also given a vision.

How I would respond to Jesus when he asks, "What do you want me to do for you?"

November 5

Thirty-first Sunday in Ordinary Time

Macrina Wiederkehr, O.S.B.

Mark 12:28-34   Lectionary 152B

". . . with *all* your heart, with *all* your soul, with *all* your mind, and with *all* your strength."

According to the great commandment this is how I am to love God. The **all** frightens me. **All** is everything I have; nothing is held back. How am I to love One I cannot see with my physical eyes, in such a total manner?

As I struggle to believe in my ability to love God so completely the second commandment comes to my assistance. I am to love my neighbor as myself. Here I receive a clue as to how to love this unseen God and it has something to do with my neighbor. Another scriptural text sounds in my ear, "those who do not love a brother [or sister] whom they have seen, cannot love God whom they have not seen" (1 John 4:20).

Jesus speaks of a love that has infinite power. The way to let God rule my life is to give myself to that love. My **all** today is not the same as my **all** tomorrow. I am to love with as much heart and soul as I have at the present moment.

During this week I will ponder how I can learn to love God by loving others. Whom will I choose to love this week?

November 12

Thirty-second Sunday in Ordinary Time

Richard Oswald

Mark 12:38-44   Lectionary 155B

"She, from her poverty, has contributed all she had, her whole livelihood."

I have fond memories of an uncle who visited my family's home several times every week throughout my childhood and early adult years. He lived a lifestyle that was frugal to the extreme. He preferred to use his income to support his parish, help build mission churches, care for the poor, and to fund the education of his nephews and nieces. His generosity was more than equaled by his trust in God.

Despite the death of his wife and only child, the failure of two businesses, and the Cold War, he was always a man at peace. He responded to every situation with the words that I wish had been carved on the marker for his grave, "The Almighty still rules this world." He knew that before God he was powerless and his only response was to surrender.

I wish that I could say that I have reached my uncle's level of trust. Perhaps it will take the rest of my life and the acceptance of my death to achieve it. As I continue the journey, my uncle and today's widow serve as models for the humility and true self-awareness that characterize a disciple of Jesus.

Is my life's journey leading me to take greater steps of trust?

Thirty-third Sunday in Ordinary Time

Esperanza Micaela Espinoza, M.C.P.

Mark 13:24-32   Lectionary 158B

When you see these things happening, know that he is near.

With so many natural disasters, wars, and injustices against human beings before us, and many other things that we see each day in the news, perhaps we start to question: Are these not the signs Jesus speaks of in Scripture?

All of these sorrows and woes certainly remind us that under God's reign, things would be very different. The second coming of Jesus is our greatest hope. When will it be? Only God knows his plan, and no one else.

Nevertheless, in each moment of our lives, God is always present. The invitation is to be alert and discover the symbols, the signs, that indicate God's daily and continuous presence in our lives. A certain intimacy, and burning search is needed, to be in perfect understanding (harmony) with God. God does not allow himself to be outdone in generosity. He gives a hundredfold and will manifest his glory and his power by giving us a new reason to exist.

What are some of the signs of God's presence in my life?
Do I easily recognize the meaning of these signs?

Feast of Christ the King

David LeSieur

John 18:33b-37   Lectionary 161B

"My kingdom does not belong to this world."

While we Americans can appreciate the tradition and the panoply associated with kings and queens, we would never prefer monarchial government to our own democratic form. After all, we know what it's like from our colonial days and we fought a war to be free from kingly rule.

So today's solemnity of Christ the King may seem a little quaint to Americans, a little out of step with our 230-year experiment in democracy. Perhaps, but we honor today a ruler whose kingdom is not of this world. Jesus redefined kingship.

Pilate thought he knew all about kings; he was a "friend of Caesar"—a political title bestowed on loyal middle managers such as himself. But he didn't know about Jesus' kind of kingdom.

Pilate understood power and control, the strength of horses and soldiers. But he didn't get the notion of service and the washing of feet. Nor would he understand how Jesus put up no resistance at his arrest, telling his followers to sheathe their swords.

Those who buy into the allurement of power and control over others will not understand a kingdom based on truth, mercy, and justice for the rights of everyone, nor will they understand its King.

What does it mean to me to celebrate the kingship of Christ? Do I recognize the kind of kingdom he embodies?

Contributors

Dan Borlik, C.M., serves the Diocese of Little Rock among Spanish-speaking Catholic immigrants in sacramental ministry, intercultural communication, and pastoral leadership skills training. He is also provincial of the southern province of his community.

Peter Dwyer is the director of the Liturgical Press in Collegeville, Minnesota, where he and his family have been involved with Saint John's Abbey and its ministries for most of their lives.

Esperanza Micaela Espinoza, M.C.P., has served as director of Hispanic ministry for the Diocese of Little Rock, as well as previous service as a pastoral minister in Dallas, Texas, and Monterey, Mexico. Sister Mickey is involved in building faith communities and assisting local churches as they become increasingly multicultural.

Mary J. Glynn, S.J.C., of Galway, Ireland, has served in ministries throughout North America and has received degrees from universities in Chicago and Canada. She is the director of religious education and Christian initiation for the Diocese of Little Rock and coordinates the diocesan Theology Institute.

Roy Goetz, a deacon in the Diocese of Little Rock, is a musician who teaches New Testament Scriptures and is the director of instrumental music at Subiaco Academy, where he is also campus minister. He and his wife have two children.

Dan Hennessey is a deacon serving in the Diocese of Little Rock, a husband, the father of three sons, and a doctor of optometry. He can be seen on a number of video wrap-up lectures for LRSS.

Lilly Hess is an associate director for LRSS and has worked with LRSS for most of its thirty-one years. Among her duties she is responsible for the production of all taped materials. Lilly is the mother of four and the grandmother of nine.

Judy Hoelzeman holds a master's of religious education and is a frequent lecturer for LRSS. She is married and works as a public relations officer with a nonprofit agency that promotes the health and independence of aging citizens.

Rosa María Icaza, c.c.v.i., is professor emerita of foreign languages at the University of the Incarnate Word, and associate director of the programs department at the Mexican American Cultural Center, both located in San Antonio, Texas. She has been a primary translator for LRSS materials since Spanish materials were introduced.

Jerome Kodell, o.s.b., abbot of Subiaco Abbey in Arkansas, is a retreat director, Scripture scholar, and writer. He authored all of the original study materials for LRSS and has remained a valued advisor to this ministry.

Msgr. David LeSieur is pastor of Our Lady of the Holy Souls Catholic Church in Little Rock and is director of continuing formation for clergy for the Diocese of Little Rock. He is a frequent lecturer for LRSS and has served on its board of directors.

Susan McCarthy, R.D.C., is the workshop and promotion coordinator for LRSS. Much of her previous work has been in teaching and pastoral ministry in the Archdiocese of New York, where she also earned an M.A. in pastoral ministry. She can be seen on a number of LRSS video wrap-up lectures.

Msgr. Richard Oswald is pastor of St. Vincent DePaul Parish in Rogers, Arkansas, and serves on the clergy personnel board for the diocese. He is a previous director of LRSS and has presented a number of video wrap-up lectures.

Jerre Roberts is often seen or heard on LRSS taped materials. She is a professional storyteller and a charter member of the School of Sacred Storytellers. Jerre and her husband Bill live on the Arkansas-Texas border.

J. Peter Sartain became bishop of the Diocese of Little Rock in 2000, having previously served as a pastor, chancellor, and vicar general in the Diocese of Memphis. He is also chair of the USCCB Committee on Home Missions. *Of You My Heart Has Spoken* is a collection of his writings since becoming bishop.

Tom Stehlik, C.M., has spent the last fifteen years as a Vincentian missionary, and now serves in Arkansas. His interests include neighborhood evangelization, cultural and folk art, and playing the Mexican accordion.

Martha Elena Torres, M.C.P., moved with her religious community from Mexico to Arkansas to work among Spanish-speaking Catholics in Arkansas. As part of her parish-based ministry, she coordinates two groups of adults using Estudio Bíblico de Little Rock, and has trained local Bible study facilitators.

Mark Twomey since 1982 has served as the editorial director of the Liturgical Press. During that time he has worked with the Little Rock Scripture Study on developing new product for the program.

Cackie Upchurch is the director of LRSS and has authored study guides and wrap-up lectures. She serves as an associate editor for *The Bible Today* and has presented workshops and retreat days around the country. Cackie is actively involved in adult faith formation efforts in the Diocese of Little Rock.

Macrina Wiederkehr, O.S.B., author and spiritual guide, is a Benedictine of St. Scholastica Monastery in Arkansas. Her books include *The Song of the Seed* and *Gold in Your Memories,* and, most recently, *The Circle of Life: The Heart's Journey Through the Seasons* (co-written with Joyce Rupp, O.S.M.). She also writes "Romancing the Word" in *Stepping Stones,* the newsletter of LRSS. Macrina is a popular retreat director throughout North America. See www.MacrinaWiederkehr .com.

Gregory C. Wolfe is director of finance for the Diocese of Little Rock. In addition to an M.B.A, he also holds a B.A. in Theology and an M.A. in formative foundational spirituality and has been a frequent lecturer for LRSS. He is married and is the father of one daughter and three sons.

Clifford Yeary holds a master's degree in pastoral studies and a B.A. in theology. Among his duties as associate director of LRSS, he is responsible for writing and revising study materials, and presenting wrap-up lectures. Cliff is the author of the study guide for *Good News in New Places.* He and his wife are the parents of three children.

About Little Rock Scripture Study

Little Rock Scripture Study began in 1974 by developing materials that could be used in small groups by people interested in Bible study in Catholic parishes. In the past thirty years, over three million study sets have been used by participants all over North America and in over 50 countries beyond its borders.

The method of Little Rock Scripture Study involves daily prayer and study, weekly small group prayer and faith sharing, accompanied by a weekly wrap-up lecture. The purpose is not simply to acquire knowledge, though biblical literacy is one good result. The more important focus of Bible study is to grow in relationship with God and with the believing community.

Little Rock Scripture Study is a ministry of the Diocese of Little Rock in Arkansas in partnership with Liturgical Press in Collegeville, Minnesota. The staff in Little Rock develops the study materials, produces the taped materials, presents diocesan workshops, organizes a yearly summer Bible Institute, and puts together the newsletter *Stepping Stones,* which is published three times each year. Liturgical Press edits and publishes the study materials, designs marketing pieces, maintains the website, and oversees all orders and shipping.

For more information about Little Rock Scripture Study and the materials available for group study, contact:

Little Rock Scripture Study
2500 North Tyler Street
Little Rock, AR 72207

Phone: 501-664-0340 or 800-858-5434

e-mail: lrss@dolr.org

website: www.littlerockscripture.org